AL DI MEOLA'S

PICKING
TECHNIQUES

Executive Producer Philip Roberge
Produced by John Cerullo
Cover Art and Design by J. J. Flannery
Type Editing by Carol Flannery

Produced by Third Earth Productions
Distributed by Hal Leonard Publishing Corporation

CONTENTS

FOREWORD

My main purpose in writing this book on picking technique is to help guitar players develop speed and accuracy in their playing while developing their own musical goal. By doing this, the guitarist is better able to hear, play and write creatively for the guitar.

Many of today's guitar players, particularly rock guitar players, are limiting themselves. By not learning speed, accuracy, and scale work, they have no chance to develop a variety of styles, tempos or other important musical elements.

In order to be an effective and creative player today, a guitarist must learn the entire fretboard in a scale-wise fashion and be able to do it with speed and accuracy. An added help would be to listen to lots of different styles of music, not just top 40.

This book has been simply structured for ease of use and accessibility to every guitarist who wishes to develop his picking technique. The real secret to it all is to practice a lot and to start slowly, gradually building speed, while always playing as clearly and accurately as possible. The main thing is to work hard on repetitive rhythms—it's the only way to improve.

The outline of the book follows the development of alternate picking: first single string alternating, then work on repeated upstrokes, alternate picking on adjacent strings, and finally alternate picking skipping strings. These different elements of picking and some variations will all be demonstrated by the use of exercises, scales, folk songs, and excerpts from my own tunes. An explanation of my muting technique is also covered.

The excerpts from my own music include bass lines and chord changes for anyone who wishes to play with a friend or teacher. The left hand fingerings are those suggested by the editor and not necessarily my own. Full transcriptions of the tunes used in this book can be found along with other tunes of mine in my book, *Al Di Meola, Music/Words/Pictures*. I hope you work hard and enjoy the book.

Al Di Meola

MUTING TECHNIQUE

The muting effect is performed by damping the strings with both the right-hand palm and the fingertip and finger-nail of the right index finger while picking. The pick hits the strings first, followed by the skin of the fingertip, then the nail. Varying the amount of pressure used will alter the effect of the muting. Note: This technique is only effective on the upstroke (∨).

Another way to approach this is to strike the string with both the pick and the tip of the index finger simultaneously. This works well on downstrokes (⊓) as well as upstrokes. I find that using these techniques will make the sound of the strings project better when it is necessary for them to do so, such as in a solo. There are many different combinations of textures that one can create by muting. All it takes is practice.

When playing electric guitar, especially during a solo break, when you are using a sustain setting, your guitar will sound "muddy" when you get down to the "A" and "E" strings. It doesn't matter how cleanly you pick, it will get washed out. So many guitarists do this, and it then becomes impossible to distinguish what is being played. The muting technique will help you to play on sustain and at the same time let the note "pop" out, with a clear percussive sound and feel.

ALTERNATE PICKING

I always use alternate picking in my playing. This is the constant use of upstroke (∨) followed by downstroke (⊓), or the other way around, depending on which stroke I start the particular musical passage. I occasionally use all upstrokes or downstrokes repeatedly if it can create the right musical effect that I'm looking for, but for the purpose of this book, you should always use upstroke followed by downstroke or vice-versa. I do include a few exercises for repeated upstrokes because on guitar it is most difficult and extremely effective as a variation in picking rhythmic accents.

RIGHT HAND POSITION

As fas as hand position goes, I do not advocate any particular position. Some players feel more comfortable resting their right hand on the bridge, and others prefer a "floating" position, where the hand is free to move about. I use both techniques depending on what I'm playing.

When playing a difficult passage, you should try resting your hand on the bridge, as it gives you more stability and helps your accuracy. Otherwise, either position will do. I feel any teacher who advocates only one position is limiting the student. A player should learn both, as there are benefits to both positions, as you will see as you progress.

ARTICULATION

Articulation is one of the most important musical elements to consider, especially for the guitarist. When using the pick you must create a smooth, flowing, and properly accented musical line, no matter what type of music you are playing. Alternate picking helps you achieve this. It works naturally with most common and some not so common melodic and rhythmic phrasing. As I mentioned earlier, although I occasionally use a repeated upstroke(s) or downstroke(s) to help create a special articulation, I generally use the alternate picking style. I might start a given phrase with either an up or down stroke, depending on the character of the phrase, but I do alternate constantly. If you start a given phrase or section with a downstroke, for example, and it doesn't sound right as you go along, stop and try starting with an upstroke. Either one will usually give you good articulation as long as you remember to alternate the picking. Whichever picking you start with, it will usually be good all the way through that phrase for articulation purposes.

SINGLE STRING ALTERNATE PICKING

The easiest place to start picking is on a single string, for one reason—you can concentrate on your right hand movement. You should focus in on "economizing" your hand and finger movement in the right hand. By economizing I mean for you to try not wasting motion between up and down strokes. First start with a repeated downstroke. Stay close to the string when you start and follow through only enough to finish picking the string, then return immediately to the starting point. Try the same thing with the upstrokes, then do them both together. Start with the downstroke, follow through just enough to pick the string, then return via the upstroke to the starting position of the downstroke. Continue this pattern slowly, always watching your economy of movement. This will help you develop both your speed and accuracy. Remember, if you want to achieve this, make sure that your right hand isn't "flying" or moving all over the place. If it is, the technique won't work.

Play the following three excerpts using

1. Downstroke
2. Upstroke
3. Down-up stroke
4. Up-down stroke

They are each marked with a tempo metronome marking. This metronome marking should be your goal, but don't start there. Start slowly and evenly, gradually building up tempo. If you try to play it faster than you are capable of, you will play it sloppily, and you will always play it that way. Playing fast without any control is one of the worst bad habits you can develop, and it's one of the hardest to get rid of.

Example #1 — "Race With Devil On Spanish Highway"
Tempo — ♩ = 152 or 𝅗𝅥 = 76

Example #2 — "Casino"
Tempo — ♩ = 132 or 𝅗𝅥 = 66

Example #3 — "Egyptian Danza"
Tempo — ♩ = 116 or 𝅗𝅥 = 58

ALTERNATE PICKING
ON ADJACENT STRINGS

Now that you have learned alternate picking on a single string, you can work on moving from one string to another. Our first step will be to move to strings adjacent to one another. This is best accomplished by playing scale fragments and then playing full scales. Scales are important to learn. They are a device for learning notes on the entire fretboard, and they are the key to melodic playing. Rock players usually play with their first and third fingers only when they are improvising. As a result, you hear some very unmelodic playing. I suggest you learn scales, not riffs, so that the four fingers of your left hand can explore the fretboard. This will allow you to play and hear music in a more melodic and creative fashion. I suggest you learn all scales in all positions, such as major, minor, and modal. But for our purposes here, we will only use a few scales from the major keys.

Play the following fragments with alternate picking. Also, play them with all upstrokes while trying to get a smooth sound. Again concentrate on economy of movement in the right hand. Only move your hand enough to get you to the next string.

Example #1 — C Major Scale Fragment (II Position)

Tempo — ♩ = 120 or ♩ = 60

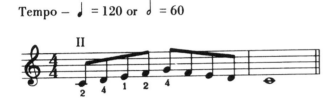

Example #2 — G Major Scale Fragment (II Position)

Tempo — ♩ = 120 or ♩ = 60

Example #3 — D Major Scale Fragment (II Position)

Tempo — ♩ = 120 or ♩ = 60

Now play the full scales, which move from the sixth string all the way to the first stirng. Again, only move your hand and fingers as needed. Don't waste motion in either hand. Start slowly and accurately, gradually building speed up to indicated tempo marking.

Example #4 — C Major Scale (II Position)

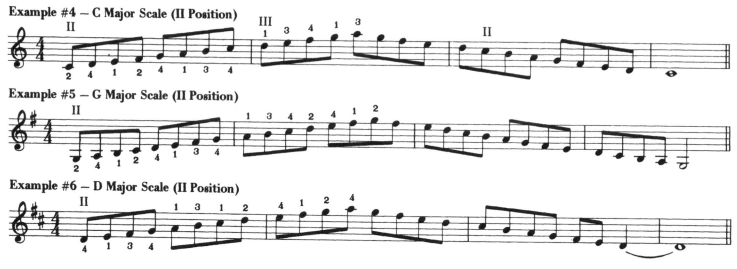

Example #5 — G Major Scale (II Position)

Example #6 — D Major Scale (II Position)

The next exercise will involve an entire tune to practice. In this tune, you should learn one section at a time and repeat it before you go on to the next section. The repeat marks are indicated for you. This piece, the "Tarantella," is a good exercise for our purposes, because like most Mediterranean folk music it starts slowly and gradually increases to a blinding speed. So practice it slowly, learning each section well, then incorporate the increase of speed right into the tune as you continue. Another example of this can be heard in one of the middle sections of my tune "Egyptian Danza."

Example #7 — "Tarantella"

Tempo — ♩ = 96 gradually increasing speed each time

ALTERNATE PICKING ON SINGLE AND ADJACENT STRINGS

In this section we will play some more complete fragments from my music, the goal still being to learn and master one excerpt at a time.

I find when a student is presented with a full transcription of a piece, he doesn't usually take the time to learn and master one section at a time. But once you learn this way, you can "string" the sections together and play the whole tune. This is why I suggest using this book first before using the *Al Di Meola—Music/Words/Pictures* book. It forces you to learn in sections, therefore learning better!

The following excerpts start with single string alternate picking and then move into alternate adjacent string picking.

Example #1 — "Casino"

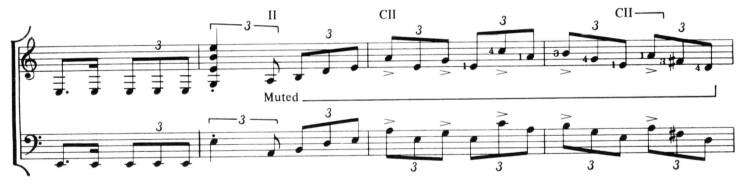

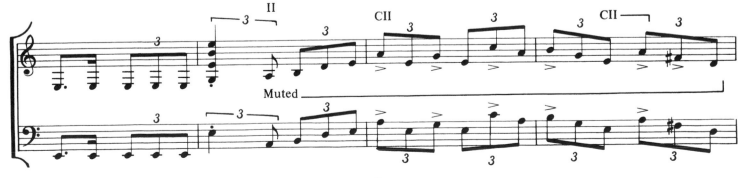

Example #2 — "Race With Devil On Spanish Highway"

Tempo — ♩ = 152 or ♩ = 76

Very fast

ALTERNATE PICKING ON EASY SKIPS

Alternate picking with skips involves the movement of the pick from one string to another with the skipping of a string or strings in between, such as moving from the sixth string to the fourth string, or the fourth string to the first string.

In the following example, we encounter a skip from the second string to the fourth string. Practice this type of picking as much as you can. This technique will help you in creating better and more varied melodies, as you can incorporate melodic skips into your playing and writing.

Example #1 – From "Elegant Gypsy Suite"

Tempo – ♩ = 184 or ♩ = 92

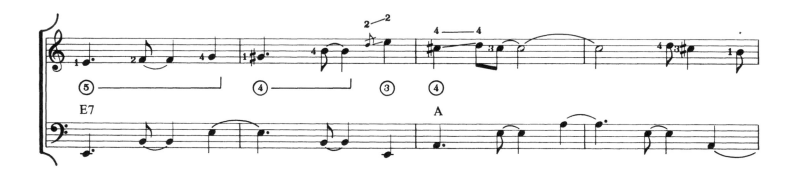

14

In this next example you can practice playing a scale-type passage, which includes an interesting melodic skip phrase. This adds greatly to the feel and mood of the melody.

Example #2 – Excerpt from "Egyptian Danza"

Tempo – ♩ =126 or ♩ = 62

ALTERNATE PICKING ON CHORDS

Adjacent Strings

Chordal playing in a picking fashion is something that too few rock, pop, and jazz players learn. If used properly, the pick can produce beautiful picking patterns on chordal passages. The trick is to practice them enough, trying to produce as smooth a sound as you get when playing with your fingers.

In this first example, play the "Guitar" part first instead of the "Solo Guitar" part. This section for the accompanying guitar picks a chordal passage on the first three strings. Practice this with a steady right hand. Learn the notes well before you try to worry about picking it smoothly. It's always harder to pick notes smoothly when you are stumbling over what notes to actually play! Use alternate picking all the way. Later, practice the solo guitar part as well. As you can see, it contains slides for the left hand on certain notes. This is another technique I use quite a bit. It involves picking the first note then sliding up to the next note without actually picking it. This creates an interesting effect that is used a lot in Mediterranean music.

Example #1 — Excerpt from "Electric Rendezvous"

*Acoustic Guitar Solo

16

Skipping Strings

      In this next example, we have a continuation of example #1 from "Electric Rendezvous," except we now must skip strings between notes. You may start with either an up or downstroke. The important thing is to be efficient with your movement in the right hand. If you waste motion in between striking the notes, you will lose valuable time in executing the entire passage with smoothness, speed, and accuracy. Again, the accompanying guitar is the part to concentrate on. The solo guitar is present in the excerpt and can be practiced with the focus on the slides.

Example #2 – Excerpt from "Electric Rendezvous"

Tempo – ♩ = 144 or ♪ = 72

* Electric Guitar Solo

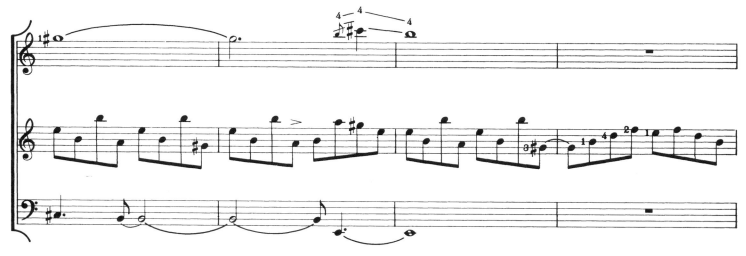

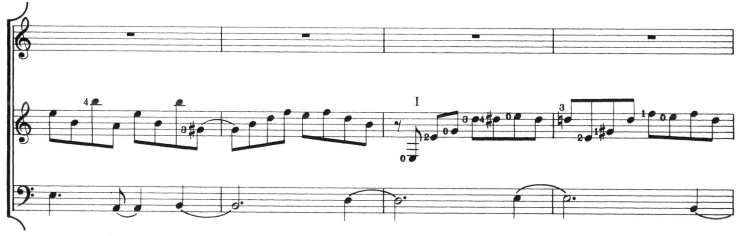

SUMMARY OF TECHNIQUES
LEARNED SO FAR

So far we've discussed a number of techniques which are signatures of my music, as well as general technical points for anyone who wishes to learn to pick better. Instead of a verbal review of the points we've considered, let's use a musical example to show how I incorporate all of these devices into a single section of a tune. See if you can identify all of them, as well as play all of them! This particular section will also show you a new element—the use of the triplet. Most of the triplets in the example are: ♫ = ♫♪

Example #1 – Excerpt from "Egyptian Danza"

Tempo — ♩ = 132 or ♪ = 66

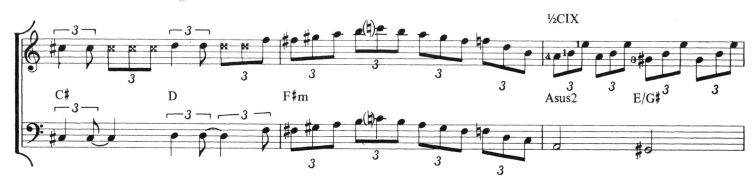

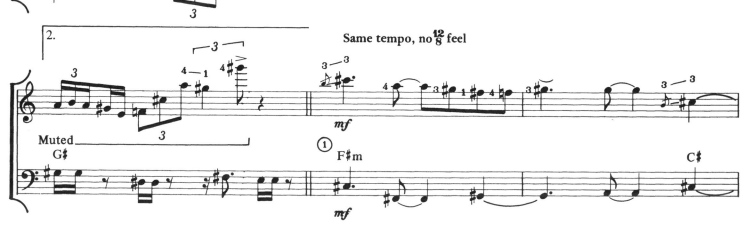

ALTERNATE PICKING ON MELODIC SKIPS

Melodic skips are so pretty and add such variety to melodies that entire melodies composed of all skips can sometimes work well. This gives quite a challenge to the right hand, as it has to constantly be skipping strings and intervals. The result is well worth the effort.

Example #1 — Excerpt from "Electric Rendezvous"

Tempo — ♩ = 120 or ♪ = 60

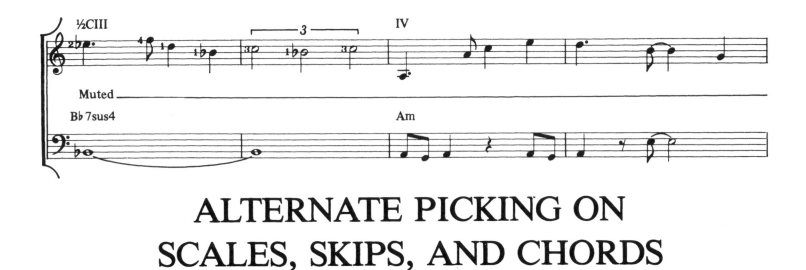

ALTERNATE PICKING ON SCALES, SKIPS, AND CHORDS

Even though these technical points have all been considered previously, the context in which these separate elements occur can vary greatly. We already saw the combined usage of all of these elements in our chapter "Summary of Techniques Learned So Far," in the excerpt from "Egyptian Danza." It is important to explore other contexts in which these different elements are combined. I suggest that you develop an ear for hearing how these various technical and musical elements are combined whenever you are listening to music. It will be a great help to your creative playing and your musical ear.

In the next example we have an excerpt from "Electric Rendezvous" in which I combine the scale, skips, and chordal elements of picking into a 12 bar phrase. It works very nicely. The chordal section (last 4 bars) is the hardest to play, considering all the skips. Start with a downstroke for the best articulation.

Example #1 — Excerpt from "Electric Rendezvous"

Tempo — $\quad \downarrow$ =160 or $\downarrow.$ = 52

MORE ADVANCED ALTERNATE PICKING ON ADJACENT STRINGS

In the following example, we explore an adjacent string alternate picking passage that is simple to play, yet difficult to execute beatwise. It has a sort of boogie beat with the accent on the downbeat (notes on the 5th string). This takes a lot of care and practice in articulating the beat. Otherwise, you'll lose the beat! Watch the slide in the 4th measure. And the last two bars are tricky; a chordal riff moves back into the transition phrase for the repeat of the entire section again. Start with an upstroke in order to help you with the articulation.

Example #1 — Excerpt from "Electric Rendezvous"

Tempo — ♩ = 184 or ♩ = 92

23

FURTHER SKIPS WITH STEP-WISE BREAK

An effective melodic picking device is to break up the melodic skips with short step-wise breaks. Musically, it's very effective, and it's a great exercise with its quick movement from skipping strings to playing adjacent strings. A good example of this is found in "Electric Rendezvous." The skips alternate with the step-wise breaks, which then progress into a scale passage climaxing at the end.

Example #1 — Excerpt from "Electric Rendezvous"

E7

½CIX ½CIX

N.C.

VI VII

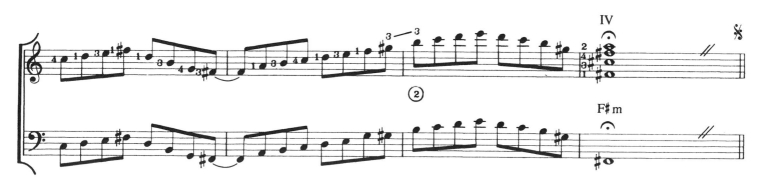

IV

②

F♯m

25

DOUBLE NOTE PICKING

Double note picking can be done with either up or downstrokes repeated, or with an alternate style. But for the best feel, at least in my style of music, I find repeated downstrokes to be the most effective. The following example shows this to be true. Watch out for the staccato double notes. They can be played by either muting the strings or cutting them short with the palm of your hand quickly after picking them. Do not mute the single notes.

Example #1 —Excerpt from "Elegant Gypsy Suite"

Tempo — ♩ = 160 or 𝅗𝅥 = 80

Example #2 – Excerpt from "Elegant Gypsy Suite"

"TARENTELLA" REVISITED

If you recall, back in one of the first chapters we used the Italian folk tune "Tarantella" as an example of accelerating the tempo each time the tune is repeated. At the end of that section I mentioned a good example of this could be found in the tune "Egyptian Danza." The following example is that section of the tune. Play through the excerpt, each time increasing the speed (as I do on the record).

Example #1 — Excerpt from "Egyptian Danza"

Tempo — ♩=126 getting faster each time

CHORDAL STRUMMING

The key to chordal strumming is in developing a quick wrist. Practice the following example always watching the up and down beat. This is usually your indication for which stroke you use: Downbeat—downstroke, upbeat—upstroke.

There is also a lot of chordal picking, so be careful. Again, with strumming, just as with picking, use economy of movement. Don't strum up or down any further than you need to—just enough to strum the strings that you want. The fingerings and positions are shown in the tablature line.

Example #1 — Excerpt from "Passion, Grace & Fire"

Tempo — $\dot{\quad} = 69$

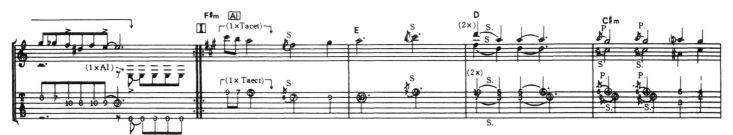

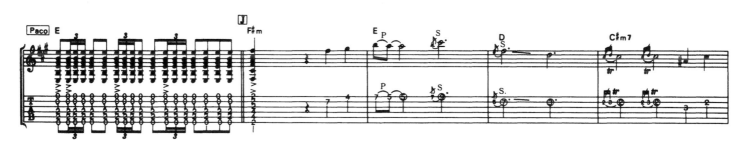

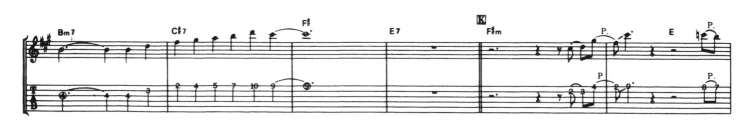

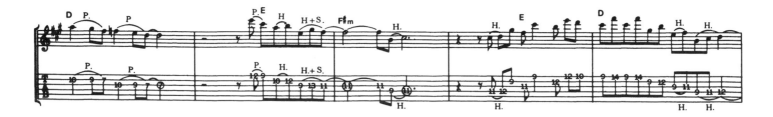